LIGHT-UP SWAN

LIGHT-UP
SWAN

TOM
SNARSKY

//

ORNITHOPTER PRESS   PRINCETON

First Edition

Published by Ornithopter Press
www.ornithopterpress.com

ISBN 978-1-942723-09-7

Library of Congress Control Number: 2021934731

Cover image by Jo Ianni & Jesse Murray
Courtesy of the artists

Design and composition by Mark Harris

for Kristi

CONTENTS

But what if the ghost is empty because it's making a space for you?

—Bhanu Kapil

THE STAR-FIELD PAINTINGS

I'm here to mail a letter
It will kill me but I don't mind

I just assumed
Corinthians were flowers

One kind of pain can hide
Another, like in one star-

Field painting of
The city there are no

Stars at all because the light
From below is too much

But in another star-field painting
From a less-lit place

That auditorium of tiny bright
Dots drowns out

Any light from below
It is easy to forget that

The stars have already solved
The problem of the one

& the many: in the day, there is
One, & at night the many sing

A work song carrying
Our oily night on their backs

Look through the hole
burned in the silk, like Laura
Dern's character in *In
land Empire*—what do
you see? A vast graveyard
stretching past the sun?
Four lanterns you forgot
to light? The present tense
is too tired to continue.
Before darkness comes,
I'll love you like a bird
(a Clark's nutcracker)
loves to remember
where she hid her seeds.

ARTIFICIAL INTELLIGENCE PAINTING

Down the April corridors we stumble,
reinventing names. The lilacs softly put.
Solfege lilting the way sadness makes you
walk, like an awkward bird in the corner
of the canvas—radiating doubt, sure, but
no ill will. When all of this darkness builds
into wind, I hope you'll have a few stock
answers to distract them, even if only
for a moment. My heroine my heroine
my little blue light. A soft rain interrupts
the grazing. No record of it anywhere.

WISH

My trick is to pretend
To be a person you might want
To know
In the initial stages
& then to fail
At being that
In a million small meticulous ways
Until our century
Finally passes

EVEN WITH ADVANCED AIR BAGS

I think we can be worried
that time won't be enough
of a deterrent. Sitting like
a gargoyle atop the present
& all its terrible fears, I feel
the way a laundromat might
when the bank finally stops
rolling quarters. I think we
made a more powerful enemy
than we thought when we
started disrespecting death,
acting like it was so familiar.
When the music box opened
& nothing came out, not even
the silent glint of its metal
crank, the idea shot forth
unbidden that we might need
to leave here for a while, to
find someplace safer. It all
hinges on the ability of love
to pick up its million stained
pieces & leave good enough
directions for how to re-
assemble them into some-
thing almost shining, capable
of music when opened into
now by a calm, firm hand.
& though I won't volunteer
for that job, I cannot wait
to grasp the hand of who-
ever does, to pull it in close
over my heart & ask them if
they feel anything—anything

at all radiating out from that
devastated little cave, lined
with my ribs from which no
good thing / was ever made.

FUNNY ZERO

I became a standup comedian
who told no jokes, only stood up
on stage and got laughed at
continuously for hour-long sets
at a time. Then I'd go back
to my dressing room, count the
minutes until midnight when
we could celebrate the birth of
a new day, arrival in a new city
on my nonstop silent tour
of America, a flashlight with
dead batteries in my backpack
for years next to a book of
poems by Julian Talamantez
Brolaski. *I'm gonna meet so
many new fire hydrants this year,*
I told myself, back in those times
before I wrote my first joke
and ruined everything

HELIUM HOOD

The stars burn in my windpipe
Just kidding, it doesn't feel like that

OCTOBER (1994)

Gray bear got you by the scruff enough lately
that you haven't put on any music for days
and you're ashamed because it's uncouth
to write the same poem forty times about
the same song, "October" by Jackson C.
Frank as recorded on (I think?) *Heartbreak
Hotel* from the '90s toward the relative end
of his life, voice mostly a mess but is that
also the one with both versions of "Tumble
in the Wind" or no? *That* song, its grip
on me as a sad seventeen-year-old up
too late addicted to approval on music fora
and feeling a flickering incipience of the sad
twenty-X-year-old I would grow to be,
complete in the sense of done seeking
at least on purpose, like standing beside
a vein to watch the deoxygenated blood
shuttle back in not-yet-desperation, how
Frank's speaker rides the flatcar or follows
the signal depending on which song
he's singing because this kind of criticism
-lite is so much easier than *living*, that's why
I slip into it like the habit of only playing
that one pathetic playlist I made with two
songs on it called Two Songs, the Webern
Klavierstück in E Minor and then "October
(1994)" announcing its year like which
black metal album(s) is that? I can google it
but let's guess *In the Nightside Eclipse* and
I hope also *Transilvanian Hunger*, great
eponymous murderer of me on Audiosurf
because like all the noise tracks I loved
it was just basically one long fuzzy assault

that the algorithm didn't know what to do
with, although it could handle the fuzz in
something like Khonnor's *Handwriting*
from Typo, another inescapable talisman
of those years, so ridiculous to live
in memories like these now, and best of all
I don't remember anything of love for *people*
during this stretch, just that deepfaked
religious seriousness I tried to give
to music then and which has now migrated
to poetry, the same way the fleas crawled
up Gus's kitten face when we gave him his
first bath in the hottest water he could stand.
A Perfect Pain was another one, the song
though was called "A Perfect Restraint"
with Masami Akita's *Tauromachine*-era
relentless loops undergirding (RIP) Genesis P-
Orridge's unmistakable voice, the closest thing
to restraint I'm dealing with now is how hard
it is for me to type all these *p*'s with just
my left hand, my right arm wrapped fully
around your shoulders in the 7AM Sunday light
and so out of commission (I typed most
of them with a thumb stretched so far
over that my purple-and-green-but-somehow-
not-Barneyish phone case dug into
my tense, overextended palm, but a few
of them along with end-of-line edits and other
cursor moves I had to do with my nose,
the screen so close all its words blurred
to illegibility, which to me is maybe the funniest
thing about writing: if suddenly the little marks
slip outside perception, or if anything else
happens to jeopardize them, bad backup
spilled tea these *p*'s are *killing* me, then what?

Do they go to the great poetry farm in the sky
which I imagine looking like that musician's
place in *Upstream Color* to graze out their
days? Is Severino right in *The Essence
of Nihilism* that we have just foolishly forgotten
how everything is *already* eternal even without
playing it 1800 times on Spotify, which like
poetry starts off being very hard
to type, top-right corner of the QWERTY
keyboard and the base of my thumb on fire
but detouring left right by a WASD sense
of home and ending all but in the middle).
Remember when we used to be *truly*
afk, away from *any* k, for long enough to need
to let people know? I'm reminded of this
because my first AIM screen name was and
it pains me deeply to admit this *A Perfect
Pain* mistaqwerty, my password
mercifully forgotten but I think it had
something to do with *blackdog* something,
one of the first pairs of words I remember
loving for its sound. You'd craft these
clever away messages so when someone
tried to reach you and you weren't there
to be interesting and charming in "person"
(thumb!) there would still be a live datum
evincing that you were those things
and would still be once you got back
from eating or doing whatever had kept you
(thumb!!) from answering. Now the closest
thing we seem to have are out-of-office
replies and the professional baggage alone
on those is enough of a deterrent I think,
having to explain to your boss your reason
for needing to be unavailable to answer

emails and other business communiqués
for a while, set the keyboard down somewhere
across vast oceans, turbulent seas
unsafe for crossing so you have to be away
from it for some time, at least long enough
that by the time (Autocorrect wanted *my*
the time there and yes, how quickly it's over
is always a surprise) you encounter it again
maybe you'll have practiced enough
to plonk out a performance of that little
Webern piano piece you love
so much, or a new tune entirely.

RETURNING TO THE NIHILISM OF MY YOUTH, I BECOME UNTETHERED FROM ALL VICTORY

At the end of a very long book I cried
out of nowhere. The ocean below
continued debating. I fell asleep in the
blue light and then I awoke in the
blue light, the very long book still on
my lap. I ran at a speed of one second
per second into the future. Nothing
unifies me with the wounded spirit, its
high call to remonstrative action.
When I lift my hand in the direction of
fear it's nakedly in the hope it might
be kissed. I told all these things to
the man sitting next to me as he slept,
in the blue light by the very long book.

DEPRESSION, DISTRACTION, & LOVE

The only rule is that the eggs can never all be in one basket. Because of all the puddles I saw a person coming toward me who looked like a ghost, floating. If they're all together in one place then who's to say you won't drop them, what with everything you're carrying. A white truck took a wide right and everyone's okay. Even if your love has one hand on the basket and one hand over your lips, gently imploring you not to doom anything, the possibility always returns, swimming up and breaking through the surface, that you'll somehow fuck up the delicate equilibrium you both have established with the basket and worse, you'll take them down with you, your love and the eggs. Another white truck, this one pulled over with its hazards on. So you find ways not to think about where the eggs are, the intensity of the love that is keeping them safe sometimes frightening you with its newness, the beauty of a feeling you don't trust your life enough to let yourself get used to. No birds in the sky this morning. There's a hope there, though, that at some point the love will scar your retina just so and you will no longer be afraid to peek inside the basket, your love at your side, to see which eggs are where—even if they are all together at the bottom of the basket, in little rows like a chorus. Amended count: one bird, not so much *in* the sky as *against* it, up in their small nest overlooking the graveyard.

🦆 [THE CODE TO UNLOCK MY FATHER]

An unknown stone fruit
Carved to the pit by your voice
Threatening simple
Insurrection
Or a bonfire of the vanities

Chase me down these suburban streets
Our screens liquefying
In the shade

I played *Dr. Mario* all night
And now my hands are tired

STARLAKE

Liking tweets like finding a path through birdsong
Letting the algorithm tell me what music

To listen to, feeding it "Silver Dagger"
By Joan Baez and even though she says "Sing

No songs"* they come anyway, forever, the
Knife in the song's mother's palm notwithstanding

I boarded a raft bound for the edge of the
World but never made it, only found water

Roiling until even the gulls flew inland
To get away from it, its simple rhythm

Too calm and lasting too long for us to keep
Up with, despite counting beats on the riptide

Being sometimes our only way to survive
*Sorry it's "Don't sing love songs" with "don't" and "love"

Almost unstressed, the music the crucial part
Of the line, over against the omitted

Command ("Don't [..] love") that "Silver Dagger"'s speaker

Ends up following by the song's envoi, a
Pushing away of the moon and stars of love

Back into the dark lake of the heart from which
They arose in her lover's chest, not yet song

But getting close enough to earn a warning
Who among us isn't terrified to think

Of one person we love killing another
The blood on the knife dripping predictably

Another metronome of salt in this poem
Already so heavily disfavoring

Sweetness

MIDNIGHT POEM

The moon buried
in its big iron dome.

No lurid details
like cicadas. Just

a night, begging
for morning's wings.

GOSPEL OF THOMAS

I'm reading the Wikipedia page for angels

You do not appear on it yet

Like waiting for the fern to flower

Holding the sumac away from your eyes

In the goat's jaws

In the lowland

So that the goat's jaws will protect you

From the secret obvious mistake

Of hitting someone mid-run of the Goat

Simulator while the Devil Goat

Mutator is applied

If you can refrain from hitting anyone

For 300 seconds you'll unlock the

Angel Goat Mutator

Jump very high make all the right acting

Choices in real time w/no notes

Angels are not omniscient but they can get to

Robot Goat and make the game bug a lot

By put to [sic] many

Azazel excusing all your mistakes

Goats will seek shelter

More readily than sheep, the Lamb of God

Doesn't like to wet its feet but

In the middle of their upland grazing

Humility rings out

Like an unexpected bell

RILKE PHONE CASE

I guess this is my version
Of the way you felt you held Louise Labé, like
You *had* to translate her
Poems into the "universal" language of
Martyrdom, working from that big
Volume of her *Oeuvres*
Published in 1887 Paris by—lol—Charles
Boy, a category maybe we both have
A strained/strange/syncopated
Relationship with. People call your
Versions "overtranslated" now, like death
Entered their country of love
But they were important enough
To be notified—

& look at how Messiaen scored his birdsong,
Scanner imperfections like tape hiss but still
Plenty of information for us to hear
Their myriad colors, the songs imbued
Wetly with them like 10,000 embarrassing tears
Or the water of which just a little
Was needed to render you in watercolor
Little Modernist aberration your eye
Looking a bruised yellow green
Blue reddish-brown (I had to ask
Kristi to be sure, colorblind as
I am, just
Like I'd ask her for some music words about
The *Louange*

To make me sound like a smarter bird
About it. Intervals, yes, & the bizarre
Instrumentation fueled by carceral scarcity

Like it was screaming *No one would do this*
This way
If they didn't have to the cello telling
These difficult truths in its almost-human
Voice are there any recordings of you
I wonder—a quick google makes it appear
Not, even though you lived
Until 1926 you were never a song
On a cylinder of wax
No nightingale
Outsang you in the flat background)

Like a complicated dress that goes
With basically nothing,
Stands almost only on its own
But of course you have to be in it
Or me,
Whatever history
Dictates through lipstick
& the kind of makeup routine
You'd manage if you were brave enough
To act, less camera & more
Commedia with its multitude
Of histrionic colors
Pouncing all Brakhage on the frame
(O how you would've understood each other)

There are no angels in Labé. The whites of
Their countless eyes could not suffice to
Contain the debate between
Folly &
Love
As it lives on in the play of color,
Its characters
Leaning toward or away from the moon

Like a giant gray (Kristi's asleep
So I had to google "what color is the moon")
Camera
Beaming down on Labé's
Brave costume
Or the light between buildings

In Sonnet 24 (go ahead go read it)
Shakespeare paints this light between
Two people, an angelology
Of distance—*where your true image*
pictured lies—& god
Can't you just imagine a
Hilbert-hotel-walk-in-closet
On the head of a pin totally stacked
With beautiful clothes Rilke your white collars
To lead the angels out of the paintings
Louise's jodhpurs her riding boots &
Rope Arlecchino's many-colored tights &
The simple outfit Messiaen
Wore to the church organ each Sunday

I don't think you ever translated William
The way you liturgized our Lionnoize rider
People like to say you & he had an
Inverted relationship
To the human, him using it to figure
The non- & you preferring the other
Direction, trying
To share the notes every other thing
On god's great supervenience ladder
Would give us in our many scenes
& *does* give us, whether we take them
Or can even read them or hear them or not,
A bird scrawling in the Angelic Doctor's script
Try it with a little more wind here

A little more blue in the eye
Kristi's still sleeping but not even she
Can help me as I google "what color were
Rilke's eyes" no one thought to write it out &
The b&w photographs are no help
Paula Moderson-Becker's portrait (I mistyped
"poetrait" first, ha) is all I have to go on
But we already learned two stanzas ago
How painters lie
They are not like birds they have
Ugly motives sometimes
Hearts that scar
& paints that, though they could mix to get
Your eye color right, might not on purpose

Full flower five the ivy climbs
Five stories not a single overlapping
Plot line node petiole axillary bud
buriest thy content I didn't know
Those little Koch snowflake spikes
On the leaves were called teeth
They chew through landlords' mortar
Admirably & the birds eat the bugs
Spider mites aphids scale & mealy
Feeding on the leaves pretend we
Needed any more than soap & water
To rinse off the mites a certainty
I think you would've loved baptism
Of lighter underside & stomata

& clean bird feet from which to pitch
A song
Yvonne
Loriod's XIV. *Regard des anges*
From the *Vingt regards*

New stars falling like hammers
Trombone flames of angels ripped through
With jealousy
Not having been trusted with love
The greatest eccentricities of which
Are a letting-be
Of the music in your bird head
Your bird head
d. 17 May 2010

GREEN AND GOLD

By definition, we do not entirely know what to expect of ourselves.
—François Laruelle, tr. Robin Mackay

Gold flecks in the green water
Turning over like obvious leaves
Unstuck from the bedsheet & folded
Into a dull flame on your arm
Glinting into music too late to pause
From dances living in a city night
Warm light doesn't tell you anything
About provenance, about the darkened eye
Taking you in from the street
& offering you a scent of winter,
Ragged & fair, close to the ground &
Moving like a deathtrap toward
The beautiful—a lie not held in
By the garden's esteem, touching your face

NEGATIVE AFFECT

Just me and the ghost, bartering
fruit for moons. Waxing gibbous and
waxed flavedo, paraffin, Pierrot
forgetting which way means wane.

LOVE POEM WITH NO WORDS

This poem happens in an actual lake.

There are no words in it, only things

Burnt out of their ordering. Like a

Bright yellow prism of sunlight,

Or maybe a pearl. Things with no

Human form. Things that say sorry

When they don't have to. Like water,

Or maybe a used airbag. The fore-

Most criminal in my life is me and

The foremost healer in my life is

Indisputably you. We're in the lake

Together and it's raining. The air-

Bag full of pearls has sunk to the

Bottom. The sun is almost here.

GARDENBACK

Things pass from me
To you. I am as naked &
Without down as you were
When you came into the
World, vulnerable,
Melancholic, correctly
Unfamiliar with love. Nothing
Anymore can be simple
Between these, our
Economic bodies—but
The figs will still be here,
Safe, when night falls.

EDEN

Mirrored in a mountain river
beyond the browning underbrush,
a blue whistling thrush sets its song
to dusk's complicated music.

> Her hand almost covers the sound
> hole of the guitar as she plays.
> Broken chords eclipse that circle
> of distracted breath (not to scale).

Today, the oracle foretold
the death of fire. The flames will be
eyeless in the gladdening smoke.
Both modes sew a murder of air.

> This poem has one character.
> We'd need to go all the way back
> to Spinoza—maybe further—
> in order to find her true love.

Groups *are algebraic objects*
determined by four axioms.
They are sometimes represented
with diagrams called **Cayley graphs.**

> For a long time she has wanted
> a child. She second-guesses this
> sometimes, like anything, but her
> doubt is planar—an afterthought.

Incised into a one–time pad,
an account of the genesis
of history. The key jangles
on its ring at the bailiff's hip.

The idol lies cold on her palm.
Its metaphorical logic
twists like a balloon animal,
with crossings at faith's boundary.

Astronomers are still puzzled
by Jupiter's winds; no model
for the Jovian atmosphere
can explain all we see in it.

Random walks through the multiverse
with the Mad Hatter can help some-
times, unless she's just looking for
a quiet place to count her dreams.

Definition: *we say a group*
*is **sofic** if its Cayley graph*
is subamenable. Sofic,
from the Hebrew word for finite.

She sees the uncanny valley
from the citadel. It's unclear
why symbolic authority
is twinned in this nuclear dream.

Hellfire, plus a philosophy
of affirmation. (Furtive chance.)
Reactions, but not reactive:
the whole bright universe at once.

Ineradicable, the swerve,
completely. She stares at the list
of calculations. *Completely*
ineradicable, she smiles.

Schnittke did not have to explain
himself. He was not on trial.
Except when he was. When he was
on trial, he did not use words.

She can't see Jupiter from here.
She builds deep and shallow models
in her dreams, where uncertainty
gleams like wax fruit or red metal.

All sofic groups are **surjunctive.**
This means the Garden of Eden
theorem applies: we can look
for twin states instead of gardens.

Her copy of *Tristram Shandy*
has two folded pages: the black
page for poor Yorick, and the page
where Tristram is finally born.

The theologian broke his arm.
He rested it on the surface
of the water while he waded
further out, toward the island.

Does she really want to make him
kill the shadow man? Jupiter's
core accretes from too far afield.
Her questions are becoming gray.

Twins *are states that map to the same*
successors. **Gardens of Eden**
do not have predecessor states.
Twins are much *easier to find.*

She has overheard the March Hare
flinging snowglobes into the past.
The clock tower's going berserk.
She feeds into it, listening.

It doesn't matter how the truth
is spelled. Field above the warren.
Low grasses. Creeping rootstalks of
turmeric.   *(Dissimilation.)*

She holds the seraph in her hand.
The firmament has never felt
this real. Like royalty, she slides
her arm into the filmy sky.

Idealizations, then shock.
High Jupiter recalcitrates.
A blighted model theory
of hemlock, deathly recursive.

The vacuum throat—malfunctioning—
throws her into ruins built of
marble. A shuffled voice crackles
into the dusty, bleak sculpture.

In the year 29 CE,
on November the 24th,
a total solar eclipse was
visible near Jerusalem.

Her solar wind beckons the font
into new, unworded grandeur.
Without a preconceived grammar,
she is free to remake the voice.

Sofia Gubaidulina.
I owe you more than everything.
Sofia Gubaidulina.
Born three years and one month too soon.

Emerging from the noisy mud,
the revenant opens her eyes
and reads backwards: her blue hymnal
the softest palindrome in time.

The Dormouse cries in his sleep too.
He hides his icons in the fog
of the teapot, hazy with dreams,
yearning like a warm theory.

She drank in the immensity
of the heavens and vocalized
a rosebush. Little else took place
after that, except the birth of—

JEAN-JOSEPH SURIN WINS THE SPELLING BEE

Perdition: P-E-R-D-I-T-
Ion, Townsend avalanche,
Gravity current snowslip,
No-slip condition's exception,
Downgrade to the no-
Penetration condition, more
Free in parallel, resolving in
Parallel keys, gin & tonic,
Sloe gin, slow to begin,
J. J. Surin, covered in shit
& calling to God, in real life
& in Penderecki's opera.

IMITATION FLOWERS

How they sit on water, the vessel
brimming with it like a child with a lie.

The air, their merely being there
pushes them along, makes little ripples
fan out over the surface,
like the lie's caught on.

SEAGREEN SATANISM*

All of it was a strategy for displacement, nothing
More. Embarrassment was far (but not too far)
From its mind; I have a witness in the wings & he
Can be brought to bear on almost anything, for a
Price. We have entered deceivership and the re-
Sults are every bit as ugly as Father's Day. Don't
Worry, I've been told medicinal herbs this size
Are normal, at least at this age. When his tem-

Per has calmed check with me again and I'll let
You know about anything I have that might help.
Passionate chance might have to take it from
Here: I am worried that the laundromat will act
As a third pair of wings, but this groundless fear
Emerged only yesterday from the heat of a dream
I had about John Ashbery. There's no sense in
Arguing about it now—at least, not until sunrise.

*title taken from the French of René Crevel,
after a Robert Desnos translation by Timothy Adès

CARITAS GEMINI

I.

The dog sprinted full-bore into the field &
Was gone forever from the present tense

He turned into a stack of love letters
Scribbled on postcards with addresses
All over the world but mostly in Europe
To be read by whoever found them

Actually they were music boxes with
Nothing written on them at all
Each one a shrine to claustrophobia
& the cleverness needed to write music

II.

My reology is just a smooth pear
I first saw under a prescriptive light
In a nightclub full of people I loved &
None of whom had yet learned my name

They were all mauve without apology so
I dripped out the door & into the night
Singing their songs in my cracking voice
Until I found a dirt path that led to a field

With the redundancy of color & with love
I ran into it headlong like a black hearse

You can't spell *problem*
without *poem*

& also some rubble
to sift through

LOVE POEM COMPOSED UNDER THE INFLUENCE OF KEIJI HAINO'S *I SAID, THIS IS THE SON OF NIHILISM*

& there in the marbled timeline we each extended a branch
      to the empty
Tomb, inviting love
To decompress over the hills. His fat tongue & dark hair
      were equally
Inexcusable, but not to me. I didn't listen
When his sovereign silence importuned me
With its questions, their insane detail
Accreting a report to be inscribed on the plastic case of a
      budget drone,
Flown up & up until its innards froze & it fell relentlessly
Into the sea.

Sight gives a birth but takes it back. The chaste maroon
He knew me for was a neon sign I'd switched off. I couldn't
      maintain
The underside of a leaf—that lighter
Green, shaded & veined,
Riddled with stomata (from the Greek στόμα, *mouth*) that
      must remain open
To the air & its poisons
To give water.

SONG

You love me like an eave
Feeding rain to the gutter

I love you like a gutter
Fielding rain from the eave

SAUGUS IRON WORKS

Thinking of all the good things
you could've done but didn't
or—worse—could do but don't,

the world feels like a hand
extended to you in a dream, like
God's hand in that painting

only it has one of those joke-
shop buzzer things in the palm
and you're weirdly sensitive

to them ever since the boy
you liked in elementary school
(you had no idea) got one

with his Scholastic Book Fair order
and got you with it after he snapped
the flip-phone calculator you got

with yours you thought was so cool
—he never seemed all that broken
-up about it either, and it'd take

you years to recognize that
indifference as a kind of fatal
attractor that would lead you down

dark corridors for most
of your early life, and it does
that even now when you're not

looking or being your best
self, when your guard is
dead outside at his post and

you're so drunk you're smoking
cigarettes and the world feels
like the party in *Morvern Callar*

a procession of woozy images
where you hardly know anyone
except the man with the spotlight

and you only know him because
the comfort of abstract nakedness,
the thrill of showing strangers

fragments of your soul
like bits of shell on a beach
washing back and forth so

intently they almost seem to be
doing it on purpose, is a way
to know someone or a way to

understand yourself
when something as banal
as introspection fails,

and not *fails* as in *fails a test*
but rather the way a bank fails
to uphold the common good,

another in the long line of broken
calculators. Ariana Reines has
spoken of the pawn symbol (this:

)

as being an international glyph
for bad math (I paraphrase)
and it's so frightening how much

devaluing happens to us
but also is a thing we do
to each other, and as I typed

"is a" two lines ago
Autocorrect changed it to "USA"
being American as being

indefinite if you're lucky.
My wedding ring says "our
checkered fortunes so lucky"

(cf. Ashbery's "Instead of Losing"
as printed in *Quick Question*)
and Kristi's ring says "our

checkered fortunes so pretty"
(cf. Ashbery's "Instead of Losing"
as published at Poets.org).

This is an attempt
at the opposite of devaluing,
etching bits of poems into platinum

for love

BISEXUAL DREAM

You wake up one day
& no one knows who you are

SAMUEL

I am older – tonight, Master – but the love is the same –

—Emily Dickinson

Quel mystère
The history of bodies
Tapping on glass

A single bright lever
Pulled to dispense

Food & my
Cup is empty
Of any warning

Here in this many-
Chambered dark

Sixteen stars

The lake mist builds
Into a late word
Its song all stolen
From the cormorant

We both close
Our eyes during

Sex & imagine
Stripped birches

                                    The clear
                                    Chalice sinks
                                    In the clear water
                                    & disappears

It is amazing
This forgetting

The flatness
Of its desert

How it turns
So quickly into

Individual
Glinting grains

You look like
A sad house

—Piglet,
To Eeyore

Artless &
Doing harm

Wet memory

Sixteen stars

The deer leapt

From your head
In green silence

They touched the
Deer in my head
Softly

Before breaking

Lone horse curled
Up in the snow

A sad house

Knowing helps
Us pick the
Bitterest fruit
Like building
A new
Factory on
Burnt Factory Rd

As rain levels
This holy ground

So love levels
The black space
Between stars

                                        The light, isolate

                                        Cleanhearted

                                        & fine

WHOLESOME GHOST

After seeing the hole in the bottom
of this heart I borrowed from a man
& turned into a murmuring ocean,

I thought maybe I might be in love
with the receding tide, how I knew
it would be back in twelve hours

& twenty-five minutes, enough time
to learn a dance I have never seen
the steps for, or at least the idea

of it, how it would look if you did it
with some nameless partner on
a dark stage, the house lights out

of time to intervene—it begins &
you're already spinning, trying to
catch the specter in the corner

of your eye that can never stop
moving, since otherwise you'd see
it isn't really there & struck

with this revelation you'd forget
about the tide, inching hourly back
up the shoreline / to claim us both.

CLASSICAL

I'm still trying to remember the name of that light sculpture
Omeed and I went up all those steps to see in Pittsburgh.
Our bedroom window right now kind of looks like it, in
that I'm unsure whether our bedroom window is actually
any brighter than the surrounding dark or if I just expect
it to be. I also still feel like I'm floating on the river from
earlier, listing a little left like the kayak did for hours, which
adds to the overall aura of uncertainty. And now I've lit
up my phone to type this so even to get an idea of it again
requires stopping, letting my eyes adjust anew in the dark
for a few minutes, which since my phone is locked feel like
an eternity. I'm not really looking to resolve the question
of if the bedroom window *is* lighter or not; it's more like
I'm enjoying the slowness of the experience. I really liked
Omeed, the way he was willing to do what the signs said to
create the conditions under which the light sculpture was
intended to be viewed. The good faith that took, like when
you capsize and you trust your paddling buddy to come
over and help you not to lose your stuff or take on excess
water. Although, in honoring your togetherness pact by
coming over, if they're new like you they might not be able
to help much. Or they could capsize, too.

WIDOW CODE

I mistook your body
For a flood & died in it

Every decision is insane
N'oubliez pas ça

The secret admirer
Walks out from the mist

& takes you
As his only prisoner

You have four options
None of them are pretty

ALL PARTIAL EVIL

I am going to get to listen
to the Merzbow/John Goff
split 7" when it gets here
Friday, and I'm so excited
to add it to the list of stuff
that has felt familiar, or
maybe I should say hasn't
felt like *work* for my head,
just dropping into a groove
that's already there, as
long as you stay on Side A
(Side B of the Merzbow/
Goff split is blank), which
consists of one track
called "Untitled" and it
sounds a lot more like a
band of troubadours than
a standard noise track,
like when Masami Akita
visited the USSR and they,
after hearing one night
of his music, told him noise
wasn't going to *play*, that
he was going to need
to use real instruments
for his second night's set,
which is how we got *I'm
Proud By Rank of the
Workers*, his live album
recorded in Khabarovsk,
CCCP on March 23rd
and 24th of 1988, and
maybe there's at least

one baby was conceived
as a direct result of one
or both those sets, I'll
never know but it's fun
to imagine—your parents
so jazzed up with the
power of experimental
music that they lose it
in and through each
other's bodies, and nine
or so months later, as
Merzbow is releasing
his album *Flesh Metal
Orgasm,* you are born—
thirty years after the fact
(or not) I get to posit this
fictional person, whose
life would maybe have
been not all that different
from mine, as a unique
privilege that is mostly a
function of the way light
creeps through my
bedroom window on
Sunday mornings, gives
me plenty of time to wait
for feeling to take shape,
for the needle to swing
across the grooved side
of thinking, stop just
over the day, and then
drop like the vocals
in the track that opens
Ensemble Unicorn's
Music of the Troubadours,

a song called "Tant
M'abelis" written by
Berenguier de Palou, the
title of which roughly
translates to "So Much
I Love" and although
it starts like it's going to
be a list of all the things
the singer loves it
later becomes clear the
"So Much" is more of
an *intensity,* as the song
quickly pivots to being
about how the singer
could have anything and
everything his heart
desires if he only had
the love of the song's
addressee, *ja d'als amors
no'm pot far mon plazer,*
did I mention the whole
Merzbow/Goff split track
is built on a loop, for
nine minutes and forty
seconds it's mostly one
discernible bagpipe
melody repeated and
overlaid with the noise
you might expect but
now I'm not even sure of
that bit, I'm relying
on memory and it has
been so long since I
heard it, the only way I'll
know for sure is when I

play it as soon as it gets
here on Friday, four
days after I see you for
the first time in months
and I know we've been
keeping in contact
since then but to see
you, *really* to *see* you,
will be something else
entirely, an Ornette
Coleman feeling—don't
let me bore you with
more music, just tell me
how you've been
and let me hold
your gaze for like
maybe over the course
of the whole day say nine
minutes and forty seconds
total so I can go home
and remember it well
or just well enough
and long enough to
use something thin &
sharp to carve it
into Side B
of my heart

LAVENDER TOWN

You tell me a spell to get the ghosts
off my back. It works for a while.

Every laundromat in town is hidden
by signs that say *closed, moved, new*

location. To be warm and clean and
have time for song is a big secret.

Be careful / not to look at it too long.

🦆 [There's a creek in my veins that, when]

There's a creek in my veins that, when
It opens, spills naked salt water up the IV
Tubing to the idiot future we are making
Right now. Death is a too-big tunic I

Forgot to return so now I have to keep it
In the back of my closet for a long time.
The usually-loud guitar string is quiet.
I am shaking its legs so that they don't

Turn blue. I keep reading Noelle Kocot
Because it's important to assemble
A little bouquet of necessary poetries for
Surviving this time. That's right, it's still

Right now and we are no closer to being
Able to pull off that tunic, no closer to
Restringing, or even retuning, returning,
Crawling right into the center of the sun.

MUSIC FOR TRUE ROMANCE VOL. 1

Completely forgotten how to begin
Jealous of the ocean, how it never has to
Switch tabs out of embarrassment
For not knowing what to riddle this with

PAST THE FIREHOUSE

I can't believe the world
gave us things like *promises*
& *love* instead of just letting us

die, can't believe it gave us poems
that don't match their titles,
or trees whose leaves never fall

off unless they're alight &
getting hosed down
by volunteer firefighters

MORAL DESERT

Laura Jensen's blog is called
spice drawer mouse and her avi
is a selfie with her flip phone

I long for this Game Boy
Advance SP energy renewable
battery pak no one start yet

damn I still have all these CD-Rs
left even though I used
like 40 to burn everything I had

by Lil Wayne for a stupid
reason at least I gave them
away no one need know

about the hours I spent
nor that this act was just
a placebo for the music

I wanted to burn and give
to *you* instead your whole face
your body on the roof with me

your mouth full of ropes

CASTLE OF DARK ILLUSIONS, [FIEND/EFFECT]

First the drawbridge falls & crushes my head

Then when I respawn I drown in the moat

Two of my hearts are just outlines now & I'm

Underwater from the start this time

But I get tangled down in the loose weeds

& drown anew

Three hearts outlined & they put me in a forest

Lightning & falling trees don't get me

But the wolves do

I'm up in the turret with four hearts empty

This spawn point doesn't make any sense but

I'm too hopeless to put up a fight

The NPC is hunched over a mystery box

When I go to look inside they turn

& stab my face

& I respawn with no weapons at the bottom

Of the same dark spire a

Spiral stair spools down to me & I climb it

Now I lose a heart just from fear

I don't even have to die this time & don't know

How few I have left but less

Than halfway up the stair a spike triggers

Shoots straight out from the wall through my

Heart & I respawn again in a great hall

Of armors & weapons none of them

Mine I am still unarmed & I take

Barely ten steps before the poleax

In one armor's arms falls

I respawn on a tiny island in the middle

Of a lake nothing but fog & water all around

I'm wearing the armor whose poleax

Slayed me it's so heavy it's making me sink

In the soft dirt I try

Swimming but it's just more sinking

Through the green water into even softer dirt

This heart outline is

Worse to earn because I just have to wait for it

I respawn finally in a chamber of gold

Barred behind by a platinum door

Two hearts left full

The NPC is here

Hooked up to an iron lung

A golden lung

Their body doesn't move

Their hair is thin & limp

shallow

shallow

shallow breaths

You have two hearts says the voice

Coming from within

The chamber of gold

Will you give one of them now

It doesn't take anything to say yes

No special input

Another heart outlines & the machine whirrs

The NPC's eyes open slow on the golden table

They look over at me sadly

& say thank you

I have one life left too

But maybe you didn't know

Color returning slowly

To their cheeks

It takes one more to open

The platinum door

This fact hangs like an executioner

Hanged by another

Executioner

The voice within the chamber of gold is silent

The air is a mystery box

We look at each other in the quiet

Faces crimped with pain

& well-lit in the gleam

From the platinum door

Platinum yeah

I remember

Platinum

The forever metal

WATER TASK

with a first line by Sarah Wyman

Warm months up in an eggplant-colored treehouse

The future is sadder than the sexual marketplace

Forgotten / unafraid / one in being with the elderflower

A flour-dusted hero, blackout drunk, on his way to the new
      year

What I'm saying is that rain is not experience

It is gloves and heavy-handed verse—

In this performance art thing I'm working on

Everybody in the city with a music tattoo goes up

In front of a concert pianist

(The concert pianist is Mr. Field from Kate Kilalea's novel
      OK, Mr. Field)

And the pianist plays all the music tattoos in sequence

The performance happens only once

It is not recorded, nor is it repeated in other cities

It is something we get to hold for just a while in our living
      memory

Like a joke you know so well you can tell it

Differently each time and still get a laugh

Outside together with the night like a chalkboard, the stars
    unerased

And the embers in our fire pit forgetting how to flicker

HOLOFERNES

I kneel down in the soft dirt.
Nothing passes through my mind.
I am one

ordinary shadow, too drunk to keep myself
alive. Drunk on virtue, like Baudelaire
said—my heavy heart

could bring down this whole tent,
a big disaster circus,
every animal in it

finally free

OPERA

It doesn't feel like anything, the lead sang

RESERVOIR

I'm painting the light with one hand
Tied to a moonlit fencepost at the

Corner of this blurry field, where
Shadows throw their voices like

A hidden meaning hoping to stay
Hidden. The other side is water,

Still as an unmade wish, a surface
For your song to carry over as you

Sing to keep the time, to keep the
Time from running out into the field

& away from here, from my bound
& restless hand, so far from yours.

CASTLE OF DORK ILLUSIONS

The moon will last
Longer than any human love

I don't know if it will
Crash back into the earth eventually or what

You ever spend your whole life
Not knowing things

A consummate dumbass
W/a heart of gold

EPISTLE TO HANNAH VAN BINSBERGEN ON 4%

I thought I had precious little time
To write this but then I found a charger

Nvm
This accessory may not be supported. So

Hannah I might only have a few minutes
To tell you how much I have needed

Your poems, when I was a little baby
Poet "in those wonder years

I studied magic" (from your poem
"Voorspellingen van Julia en Sylvia"

Translated by Lodewijk Verduin and
Mia You) I can't believe (3%)

You and Ben Mirov both have poems
That end in invocation of 1998

When you and I were both five
Still looking at the world in Louise

Glück's (Nobel yay) helpful bifurcation*
And the wind had not yet blown

Us over we had not really yet begun
"To search for consistency in the wounded

literature / of everyday life" (ibid.)
Though I write this to you on the same

Day (Oct. 12) Matthew Shepard
Was killed in that same year

Sorry if I'm writing like I know you
You have every right "to

keep violence at bay" (title poem tr. Hutchison)
I know there's an unfair intimacy when

One party has read the poetry of the other
A fangirling of the heart and mind (2%)

Almost destined for projection
With everything else going on I don't

Want to put that on you
You've got your own stuff you need

To think about "there is a hollow in my heaven"
(From "Waar het Bloeit en Blijft Bloeien"

Translated also by LV & MY)
I'm just guessing at the capitalization

Of the title case in Dutch I was clearly not
Qualified to attempt the translations

I tried with Vincent of your poems
He was so patient even though my copy

Of *Kwaad gesternte* never made it over
The Atlantic so we only sojourned

Four of the poems whose full texts were
Available online (1%)

Trawling *Samplekanon* and listening
To your readings on the *Poetry*

International website
The folks from the Dutch Foundation

For Literature were so gentle
In their assassination of our attempts

Drastisch fout
But not everywhere

God I hope Sophie Collins or someone
With a translingual ear for Dutch

And English brings out the whole
Of *Kwaad gesternte,* I've never been able

To read it as a whole book and it kills me
Not to get to see the star

Motif play out across the collection
"While I was still a distant star" (back to

Julia en Sylvia, like naming yourself one
Of the Seven Sisters)

Cold & glowing like the Glück of
Faithful and Virtuous Night

I want to count you among those Pleiades
Who know how to make a book of poems

Sing, and though I lack
The book in my hands or any authority

To make such pronouncements I'll
Claim it anyway following the VSB

Kwaad gesternte is one of our finest
Duplicitous meteors

Masquerading in paper as a printed thing
Though of course it lives foremost

In the arc of its light

*childhood/memory

THE ONE AND FINAL PAIN RELIEVER

Board the raft and leave
the experiment. Tell no one
where you're going. If

they ask, give them reason
to believe you're seeing
a show on ice, the skaters

perfectly ept and the
concessions so comically
expensive you can't afford

them now, not a single one.

AFTER GERHARD RICHTER

Do you know who Geneva Jackson is?
Have you been made aware
of her ham biscuits? $6.00 per plate,
$4.00 per biscuit—true art
in the American vein, or ultimately
artery, whatever, cool mist
over the mountain(s). It would mean a lot
to me if this poem's timestamp is 9:09.

UNTITLED

I could feel the thick coats of time
traffic had layered onto our afternoon,

oils gone unblended, all of them
constituting the overall shade
of the road, its cool gray owing
to the angle of the sun against the
roadside brush / at this late hour.

Painting is an extended metaphor for
sleeping, which is half of what paint does.

The other half is waiting for light.

POEM FOR ANNE-MARIE ALBIACH

"Albiach" meant you were first
blood in *Violence of the White Page:*
Contemporary French Poetry, ed. Stacy
Doris, Phillip Foss (*Tyuonyi*'s editor), &
Emmanuel Hocquard, the whole thing
free to read online with the red
gash of your one-line poem on p. 15 (more
holy to me as p. 14 of the .pdf,
I'm hopeless for sonnets)
just absolutely stopping all forward motion. In
Keresan "Tyuonyi" means "the meeting place"
like the ruin in northern New
Mexico, a five-hour drive from White Sands
navigable through Truth and Consequences
or along Ruidoso Winter
Park (I forget about the snow in NM), just a
quick 40-minute jaunt from Mescalero
Reservation. Geography, here, is a way to hide
shapes (big ones: earth,
territory)
underneath smaller ones (nouns,
verbs). Snow,
white sand, & ash all fall like
X's (minuscule) on the meeting places of
your poems—: jouez à être, *Mez*
za Voce, home.

ACKNOWLEDGMENTS

Many, many thanks to the editors of the following publications, where versions of some of these poems first appeared: the *Neutral Spaces* blog & magazine, *Binbag Press, Marías at Sampaguitas, uncle ken presents, Back Patio, Mineral, Expat, Fathomsun/And False Fire, Black Bough Poetry, Dusie, Epigraph, Boston Accent, The Argotist Online, Amethyst Review, Another New Calligraphy, aglimpseof, M58, Black Fox Lit, surfaces.cx, Wu-Wei Fashion Mag, Touch the Donkey, Burning House Press, Heavy Athletics, Sick Lit, HAD,* and *Clarke's Great Outdoors.*

I am extremely grateful, too, for the necessary detours this book took on its way to being: thru the tender improvements of Ariana Reines's teaching, under Mark Harris's keen & kind editorial eye, and in forever debt to the love & constant support of my family and my friends. Thank you all, so much, for everything.

BONUS TRACKS:

ABOUT THE AUTHOR

Tom Snarsky is a math teacher who writes poems. He is a former Robert Noyce Teaching Fellow at Tufts University and a Senior Fellow at the Knowles Teacher Initiative. He is the author of two books forthcoming from Broken Sleep in 2022: *Speaking Roles*, a collection of poetry interviews, and *Complete Sentences*, a pamphlet of poems about teaching. He is also the author of the chapbook *Threshold*, published in 2018 by Another New Calligraphy. In addition to his work in print, several of Tom's chapbooks and pamphlets can be found online as free .pdfs: *Number Among* (Epigraph), *WEAKEN* (The Argotist Online), *21 small poems* (Binbag Press), *minimal sonnets* with Jo Ianni (Ghost City Press), the pamphlet *Two Songs* (Fathomsun Press), the self-published *Two Notebook Poems*, and *With Sorrow as My Window and Forgiveness as My Shield*, one of the winners of the Boston Uncommon Chapbook Contest at Boston Accent Lit. Along with Kristin Garth he is the co-organizer of Performance Anxiety, a monthly online poetry reading series. He teaches at Lightridge High School in Aldie, Virginia and lives in Bluemont with his wife Kristi, who all this is for.